Eleanor Roosevelt

An Inspiring Life

written by Elizabeth MacLeod

Kids Can Press

To MJ Paterson-Watt, whose character, values, commitment to her family, active involvement in her community and unyielding thirst for justice in the world make her sister and colleague to Eleanor Roosevelt.

Consultants: Barbara Lindsey, Eleanor Roosevelt Center at Val-Kill; Franceska Macsali Urbin, Supervisory Park Ranger, National Park Service

Acknowledgments: Many thanks to Barbara Lindsey and Franceska Macsali Urbin for taking time to review my manuscript and for answering my many questions. I really appreciate their enthusiasm, knowledge and care.

I'm also very grateful for the assistance I received from the staff of the Franklin D. Roosevelt Presidential Library and Museum, including Lynn A. Bassanese, Director of Public Programs; Bob Clark, Supervisory Archivist; Cynthia Koch, Director; and Mark Renovitch, Archivist.

Very special thanks to the terrific editorial and design team that works on the books in this series. Chris McClymont is a pleasure to work with, as well as being a great editor. Designer Karen Powers beautifully and creatively combines photos and text. Patricia Buckley brings incredible determination and organization to tracking down the photos. I so appreciate everything you all do.

Thanks always to Dad, John and Douglas for their continuing support. Much love to Paul for his insights, help and much more.

Text © 2006 Elizabeth MacLeod

Kids Can Press acknowledges the financial support of the Government of Ontario, through the Ontario Media Development Corporation's Ontario Book Initiative; the Ontario Arts Council; the Canada Council for the Arts; and the Government of Canada, through the BPIDP, for our publishing activity.

Published in Canada by	Published in the U.S. by
Kids Can Press Ltd.	Kids Can Press Ltd.
29 Birch Avenue	2250 Military Road
Toronto, ON M4V 1E2	Tonawanda, NY 14150

www.kidscanpress.com

Series editor: Valerie Wyatt
Edited by Christine McClymont
Designed by Karen Powers
Printed and bound in China

The hardcover edition of this book is smyth sewn casebound.
The paperback edition of this book is limp sewn with a drawn-on cover.

CM 06 0 9 8 7 6 5 4 3 2 1
CM PA 06 0 9 8 7 6 5 4 3 2 1

National Library of Canada Cataloguing in Publication Data

MacLeod, Elizabeth
    Eleanor Roosevelt : an inspiring life / written by Elizabeth MacLeod.

(Snapshots: images of people and places in history)
Includes index.

ISBN-13: 978-1-55337-778-8 (bound)   ISBN-10: 1-55337-778-8 (bound)
ISBN-13: 978-1-55337-811-2 (pbk.)   ISBN-10: 1-55337-811-3 (pbk.)

1. Roosevelt, Eleanor, 1884–1962—Juvenile literature. 2. Presidents' spouses—United States—Biography—Juvenile literature. I. Title. II. Series.

E807.1.R48M33 2006   j973.917'092   C2005-907887-1

Photo credits

Every reasonable effort has been made to trace ownership of, and give accurate credit to, copyrighted material. Information that would enable the publisher to correct any discrepancies in future editions would be appreciated.

All photos are courtesy the Franklin D. Roosevelt Library with the following exceptions: **p. 3:** (typewriter) Ivars Zolnerovichs/istockphoto, (White House) Library of Congress; **p. 5:** (UN Radio) United Nations/DPI photo; **p. 9:** (women's hats, Paris, sweatshop workers) Library of Congress; **p. 11:** (bird) Courtesy National Parks Service Museum Management Program/Home of Franklin D. Roosevelt National Historic Site/467; **p. 12:** (Theodore Roosevelt) Library of Congress, (teddy bear) National Museum of American History/Smithsonian Institution; **p. 15:** (war poster, soldiers) Library of Congress; **p. 16:** (women voting) Library of Congress; **p. 17:** (wheelchair) Courtesy National Parks Service Museum Management Program/Home of Franklin D. Roosevelt National Historic Site/3042, (Roosevelt cottage) Roosevelt Campobello International Park Commission/Harold Bailey; **p. 18:** (Todhunter School) Dickerman Collection/National Parks Service; **p. 19:** (fireside bench) Courtesy National Parks Service Museum Management Program/Eleanor Roosevelt National Historic Site/28, (candlestick) Courtesy National Parks Service Museum Management Program/Eleanor Roosevelt National Historic Site/80/81, (Val-Kill brochure cover) Courtesy National Parks Service Museum Management Program/Eleanor Roosevelt National Historic Site; **p. 21:** (airplane, Arthurdale, White House) Library of Congress, (Eleanor Roosevelt and Mary McLeod Bethune) National Archives and Records Administration; **p. 23:** (angel food cake) Cheryl Powers; **p. 24:** (war poster) National Archives and Records Administration; **p. 25:** (planes) National Archives and Records Administration, (Roosevelt, Churchill, Stalin) Library of Congress, (newspaper) Toronto Reference Library; **p. 27:** (UN flag, Universal Declaration of Human Rights, United Nations delegates) United Nations/DPI photos; **p. 28:** (Eleanor Roosevelt and Helen Keller) Courtesy American Institute for the Blind; **p. 29:** (books) Courtesy National Parks Service Museum Management Program/Eleanor Roosevelt National Historic Site.

Kids Can Press is a **corus**™ Entertainment company

Contents

Meet Eleanor Roosevelt

"Everyone must live their own life in their own way and not according to anybody else's ideas."

— Eleanor Roosevelt

The author of many books, Eleanor was also the first wife of a president to publish a regular newspaper column. You can read her "My Day" articles on the Web.

Anna Eleanor Roosevelt was Eleanor's full name, but she hardly ever used her first name.

Admirable, determined, charming, tough — Eleanor Roosevelt was all of these things. For more than 30 years, she was the most powerful woman in the United States.

Eleanor had a presence that could light up a room — but she always felt she was unattractive and awkward. Strong-minded and hardworking, Eleanor had the courage to face tragedy and heartbreak bravely during her life.

With her incredible energy and enthusiasm, Eleanor forever changed the role of the First Lady. As the wife of President Franklin Delano Roosevelt, she achieved many "firsts." They included being the first president's wife to hold press conferences, to write a newspaper column and to fly in an airplane.

During Eleanor's lifetime, women's place in American society changed quickly. She became a role model for women — and men — not only in politics but also in everyday life.

It wasn't just in the United States that Eleanor was famous. She impressed people as the only woman in the first American delegation sent to the United Nations. Thanks to her many trips to other countries, she was beloved as the "First Lady of the World."

Eleanor was well known for the many ways she helped others, especially women, African-Americans and poor people. Millions loved her because she really listened to their problems and made them feel that she was their friend.

How did Eleanor become such an inspiring person? Why did she care so much about other people? What was she really like?

Most of my friends called me Mrs. R.

Most people loved Eleanor, but some thought she had too much influence on her husband, President Franklin Delano Roosevelt.

Mother, adviser to the president, world traveler, political activist, knitter — Eleanor became all of these things.

Franklin and Eleanor had six children, including one who died while still a baby. Here's Eleanor with Anna, their first child and only daughter.

Eleanor spoke out about the need for world peace and human rights.

Eleanor never bragged about her many achievements. "As for accomplishments," she said, "I just did what I had to do as things came along."

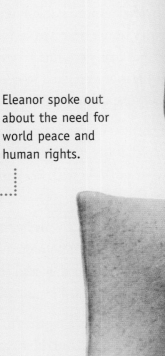

Poor little rich girl

"Looking back it strikes me that my childhood and my early youth were one long battle against fear."

— Eleanor Roosevelt

Eleanor's father, Elliott Roosevelt, belonged to one of New York's wealthiest families. "With my father I was perfectly happy," remembered Eleanor. "He was the center of my world..."

"Come in, Granny."

How Eleanor hated it when her mother called her "Granny"! Her beautiful mother, Anna, was just 21 years old when Eleanor was born in 1884. Eleanor knew her mother found her plain and serious, and she desperately wanted her mother to love her. If Anna had a migraine, Eleanor would stroke her head for hours to make her feel better.

Eleanor's father, Elliott, was handsome and charming, and Eleanor adored him. However, Elliott was an alcoholic and totally unreliable. Although the young Eleanor didn't realize it, her mother probably protected her by hiding some of the drunken things her father did.

In 1892, when Eleanor was eight, her mother died of diphtheria, a deadly disease that attacks a patient's heart, nerves and breathing. Family members sent Eleanor and her two younger brothers to live with their grandmother, Anna's mother — they felt Elliott was too irresponsible to look after children. The next year, Eleanor's brother Elliott died from scarlet fever, and a year later, her father died from alcoholism.

Mary Livingston Ludlow Hall, Eleanor's grandmother, was very strict. But she provided a more stable home than Eleanor had ever known. At the country house near Tivoli, New York, the young girl sometimes played with her many cousins. They taught her to ride, row and play games. But Eleanor also liked to spend time in a fantasy world she created. There she dreamed she was still living happily with her father.

Because of the loss of her parents, Eleanor was always scared and shy. It didn't help that her grandmother dressed her in clothes that suited much younger girls. As well, her grandmother made Eleanor keep her emotions to herself.

Eleanor's uncles also lived with her grandmother. As Eleanor approached her mid-teens, these men became more and more dangerous. Not only were they alcoholics, but they also shot guns out their windows at neighbors — and even at Eleanor and her brother, Gracie Hall.

Before she died, Eleanor's mother had said that she wanted her daughter to attend school in England. Her grandmother decided this would be a good time for Eleanor to go away. Shy, awkward Eleanor was about to become a very different person.

I was born in New York City but later lived in Tivoli, Hyde Park, Albany and Washington, D.C.

Anna Hall Roosevelt, Eleanor's mother, was very proud to belong to the Livingston family that helped found the United States.

Eleanor's brother Elliott (left) was born in 1889 but died four years later. Her youngest brother, Gracie Hall (right), was born in 1891.

The name Roosevelt is Dutch for "field of roses" and is pronounced ROSE-ih-velt.

In the photos taken of Eleanor when she was a child, she always looked solemn and sad.

"I was tall, very thin, and very shy," is how Eleanor described herself when she was growing up. She loved horseback riding all her life.

Eleanor takes flight

"I felt that I was starting a new life, free from all my former sins and traditions … this was the first time in my life that all my fears left me."

— Eleanor Roosevelt

Marie Souvestre was a wonderful teacher and an outspoken believer in the rights of women.

When Eleanor arrived at Allenswood school for girls near London, England, she was scared. Like most upper-class girls, she'd been taught by private tutors but school was new to her. Allenswood was run by a demanding Frenchwoman, Marie Souvestre, and the teachers spoke French. Luckily, when she was younger, Eleanor had a nurse who taught her French. Eleanor could help other girls with the language — and that made her lots of friends.

Mademoiselle Souvestre's goal was to turn her students into independent thinkers and politically aware citizens. She recognized Eleanor's quick mind, and the American student soon became a favorite. For the first time, Eleanor felt she belonged. Other girls valued her friendship and loyalty. Eleanor blossomed with all the time and attention she received from Mademoiselle Souvestre and the other students.

In 1902, when Eleanor was 17, she sadly left Allenswood and moved to New York City to live with some of her relatives. They believed that helping in the community was very important, but Eleanor wanted to do it her own way. While other upper-class young women sat on committees or donated money, Eleanor actually got involved with needy people.

To get experience, Eleanor joined the Junior League for the Promotion of Settlement Movements. Her work for them included teaching dance and exercises to immigrants at the Rivington Street Settlement House. Lots of the other volunteers arrived in their families' carriages, but Eleanor took a streetcar to get a sense of the neighborhood. She also joined the New York Consumers' League, which exposed the harsh working conditions of women and children.

As a member of the city's upper class, Eleanor was expected to enter society by making her "debut" in a whirl of parties. Eleanor was miserable and worried that she'd have no dance partners. She was sure she couldn't compare with her mother, who had been an exquisite debutante. Even worse, Eleanor's uncle Theodore Roosevelt was president of the United States. That meant the whole country was interested in the debut of his niece.

What Eleanor couldn't see was that she had become a graceful young woman, very tall — almost 1.8 m (6 ft.) — with lovely eyes, beautiful hair and a lively personality. A number of young men became interested in her, including her distant cousin Franklin Delano Roosevelt.

Eleanor's unhappiness at having to be a debutante shows in her "coming-out" photo.

The long hours some Americans had to work and the terrible conditions they endured appalled Eleanor.

Mademoiselle Souvestre encouraged Eleanor to buy new, fashionable clothes. Eleanor also learned to stand up straight, which made her look and feel much better.

During school breaks, Marie Souvestre and Eleanor traveled around Europe. Eleanor made all of the arrangements, which taught her to be independent.

I saw fashionable hats like these when I visited Paris.

Allenswood school for girls

Meeting FDR

Franklin Delano Roosevelt was born in 1882. In those days, very young boys from wealthy families wore their hair long and were dressed in skirts.

"Oh! darling I miss you so and I long for the happy hours which we have together … I am so happy. So very happy in your love dearest, that all the world has changed for me."

— Eleanor Roosevelt writing to Franklin

Eleanor first met Franklin Delano Roosevelt in 1886, when she was two and he was four. Years later, at a family party, he took pity on his awkward 14-year-old cousin and asked her to dance. Eleanor was very grateful.

Franklin's parents, like Eleanor's, were quite wealthy. His mother, Sara, was very protective of her only child. His father, James, had a weak heart and Franklin was told not to upset him. As he grew older, Franklin began to keep his feelings to himself, a habit that lasted for the rest of his life.

FDR, as Franklin's friends called him, grew up to be a tall, handsome, energetic young man. He didn't do very well at college, but he was popular and outgoing.

In 1902, when Franklin accidentally ran into Eleanor on a train, she was a confident young woman. She had stopped trying so hard to be what society expected her to be. Eleanor was different from the other young women Franklin knew. She was modest, with a serious side, but also had opinions and read a lot. Eleanor was interested in Franklin, too. He was handsome and loved to have fun, just like her father.

Over the next year, Eleanor and Franklin saw a lot of each other at parties and family events. Sometimes Franklin would meet Eleanor after she'd finished teaching at the settlement house. There she introduced him to a world of poverty he'd never seen.

Franklin was fascinated by this young woman from his own social class who showed him needy people and desperate situations that moved him deeply. Unlike some of Eleanor's family members, he didn't discourage her from her hands-on volunteer work.

This was one of the happiest times of Eleanor's life. But Franklin had to keep their close friendship secret from his mother. He knew she didn't want to share him with another woman. Sure enough, when Franklin and Eleanor finally told Sara they were engaged, she was shocked.

Franklin's mother asked the couple to postpone announcing their engagement for a year. She explained that it would give them time to decide if they were really in love — after all, Eleanor was only 19. The young lovers reluctantly agreed.

Franklin loved sailing during family vacations on Campobello Island in New Brunswick, Canada. He drew this picture when he was less than six years old.

At Groton boarding school near Boston, Massachusetts, Franklin joined a number of sports teams.

While growing up, Franklin had many hobbies, including collecting stamps, riding horses and snapping photos.

Sara Delano Roosevelt, Franklin's mother, spent a lot of time with him. He always loved being the center of attention.

Franklin was interested in birds all his life. He preserved this bird himself.

Eleanor felt that Franklin's mother, Sara, tried to come between the two young lovers, but she did her best to please Sara.

A new life

"I was beginning to get interested in human beings, and I found that almost everyone had something interesting to contribute to my education."

— Eleanor Roosevelt

President Theodore "Teddy" Roosevelt said Eleanor was his favorite niece. Once, on a hunting trip, her Uncle Teddy refused to shoot a bear. This story inspired a new kids' toy: the teddy bear.

Eleanor and Franklin were still in love at the end of the year. Their wedding took place on March 17, 1905. Eleanor's uncle, President Theodore Roosevelt, was pleased to take part in it. The bride wasn't surprised when her guests paid more attention to him than to her and Franklin!

The newlyweds moved into a house near Sara's in New York City. Eleanor tried to get along with her new mother-in-law. She took classes Sara recommended and gave up her charity work as Sara demanded. But Eleanor found Franklin's mother difficult. Happily, Franklin and Eleanor had no money worries. The couple received more than $12 000 a year from trust funds. (At that time, a working man earned about $600 yearly.)

Eleanor's first baby, Anna, was born in 1906. The new mother had no idea how to be a good parent, and the nannies Sara hired bossed Eleanor around. She tried almost all the advice she could get, including hanging Anna out a window in a wire box for more fresh air! Neighbors soon complained about the danger to the little girl.

James, Eleanor's first son, was born in 1907. Her next, Franklin Jr., was born in 1909. When he died later that year, Eleanor went into a long period of silence, as she often did when upset. The safe arrival of Elliott in 1910 was a relief. (A second Franklin Jr. would be born in 1914 and another son, John, in 1916.)

By 1910, Franklin was a lawyer for a top New York firm. But law bored him — he dreamed of being president of the United States. So that year he ran for a seat on the New York state senate, where President Theodore Roosevelt had also started his political life.

Franklin was charming, came from a famous family and had lots of money for his campaign. But few thought he could succeed. He belonged to the Democratic political party, and most people where he was running were Republicans. His family and party were amazed when he won.

The Roosevelt family now moved to Albany, New York, where the senate was located. Eleanor became fascinated with politics. She learned how to entertain to gather support for Franklin. With her help, FDR was re-elected to the New York senate in 1912, then in 1913 was appointed Assistant Secretary of the Navy, a very important position. Eleanor and the family made another move — to Washington, D.C.

Eleanor and Franklin had a large family. From the left, the children are Anna, Franklin Jr., James, John and Elliott.

Eleanor was upset when Franklin's mother chose the first house in which the newlyweds would live, as well as its furniture and servants.

At Eleanor's wedding, many of the guests felt that she looked as lovely as her beautiful mother, Anna.

Franklin snapped this photo of me in Venice, Italy, during our honeymoon in Europe.

Betrayal

"How do you recover from disaster? You do it by meeting it and going on."

— Eleanor Roosevelt

Eleanor knew that Franklin liked many other women and that Lucy Mercer spent a lot of time with him. But she never dreamed that her husband would betray her.

The Roosevelts became very popular in Washington. But soon there was something much more serious than parties and entertaining on everyone's minds. In 1914, war broke out in Europe. Britain declared war on Germany, and other countries joined the battle. It became clear that the United States would also be drawn into the war.

On April 6, 1917, the United States entered World War I as an ally of Britain. In Washington, social calls and parties stopped immediately.

Eleanor threw herself into volunteer work. She was often up at 5:00 A.M. knitting, visiting wounded soldiers or delivering supplies (she had to learn how to drive first). She loved meeting new people and doing any job — even scrubbing floors.

In the summer of 1918, FDR was sent to Europe to inspect American naval bases. He returned two months later, sick with pneumonia. When Eleanor unpacked his suitcase for him, she discovered love letters to him from Lucy Mercer, a secretary Eleanor had hired to help her keep track of appointments. Eleanor was devastated. She felt that the people she loved the most always deserted her.

With a broken heart, Eleanor offered Franklin a divorce. But his mother threatened to cut off all of his money if he left his wife. As well, Franklin realized a divorced man would never be elected president of the country. He decided to stay with Eleanor, and she made him promise never to see Lucy again. Still, Eleanor never really got over her pain, and the affair changed her relationship with Franklin forever.

Franklin's affair transformed Eleanor in other ways. The young woman no longer felt she had to be only an ideal wife or a perfect daughter-in-law. Eleanor began to stand up to Franklin's mother and search for new ways to express herself and use her energies.

The next year, 1919, brought more grief for Eleanor. Her uncle Teddy Roosevelt, the former president, died. Shortly after, Eleanor lost her Grandmother Hall, with whom she'd lived after the deaths of her parents. Just a few months later, Eleanor suffered the loss of one of her favorite aunts, Edith Hall.

Eleanor was now determined to live life the way she wanted to live it. But soon her life, and Franklin's, would change completely yet again.

Eleanor (standing) felt a great loss when her Grandmother Hall (left) died. Also in the photo are Eleanor's daughter, Anna (center), and Elizabeth Hall, Eleanor's aunt.

Our family spent summers at Campobello, just as Franklin's family had.

Franklin, Sara and Eleanor are in the back row. The children, from left to right, are Elliott, Franklin Jr., John, Anna and James.

Eleanor was humiliated when she realized that many people already knew about the affair between her husband and Lucy Mercer.

WOMEN!
HELP AMERICA'S SONS
WIN THE WAR

BUY
U.S. GOVERNMENT BO
2ND LIBERTY LO
OF 1917

The world had never seen a war as terrible as World War I. By the time it was over in 1918, 10 million soldiers were dead worldwide and more than 20 million were wounded.

Eleanor takes charge

Eleanor became a top leader of the Women's Division of the New York State Democratic Committee in 1922.

In 1920, women across the United States gained the right to vote. Eleanor was an important member of the League of Women Voters.

In 1919, FDR resigned as Assistant Secretary of the Navy to work as a lawyer. A year later, he was nominated to run for vice-president of the United States, with James M. Cox running for president. Eleanor began working to support his campaign. This new life didn't last long — Cox and FDR lost by many votes, and Franklin went back to his law office.

While vacationing on Campobello Island in New Brunswick, Canada, in August 1921, Franklin took a dip in the icy ocean, caught a chill and snuggled into bed to get warm. He woke up the next morning with a high fever and pain in his back and legs. Soon he was paralyzed from the waist down.

Later, doctors diagnosed Franklin's illness as poliomyelitis (polio), a life-threatening disease that affects the brain and spinal cord. For weeks Eleanor nursed him night and day. She liked to feel needed, and now Franklin needed her desperately. They did everything possible in the hope that he would walk again.

Franklin's mother wanted Franklin and his family to come and live with her at her beautiful Hyde Park estate on the Hudson River in New York. There he could be a pampered invalid for the rest of his life. But Eleanor stood up to Sara and said, "I want to keep him interested in politics … I don't want him forgotten." Louis Howe, Franklin's top adviser, agreed.

So Eleanor began giving speeches and helping set up Democratic clubs for women. Eleanor wasn't naturally good at public speaking. It made her nervous, and her warm, relaxed voice became high-pitched and giggly. But with Louis's help, Eleanor began a successful speaking career, usually talking without notes.

Eleanor kept Franklin up to date on national issues and new people in politics. Although FDR wasn't running in the 1924 election, Eleanor made sure people remembered him. She kept the Roosevelt name in the spotlight by meeting and speaking with many other Democrats.

Franklin appreciated all Eleanor was doing for him. In 1925, he built a cottage especially for her at Hyde Park. Called Val-Kill, it was the only home Eleanor ever had that was really hers, and she loved it. (See page 32 for information about visiting it.)

"Franklin's illness proved a blessing in disguise, for it gave him strength and courage he had not had before."

— Eleanor Roosevelt

Before Franklin got polio, he was an active man who loved swimming and sailing. Afterwards, he never moved again without pain.

After Franklin got polio, he spent most of his life in a wheelchair. He could stand for a short time using canes, leg braces or helpers.

The Roosevelt cottage on Campobello Island has more than 18 bedrooms!

After Franklin was diagnosed with polio, Eleanor had to be more than just a mother to her children. She wrestled with them, took them camping and learned to swim so that she could teach them.

Political insider

Nancy Cook (left), Marion Dickerman (center) and Eleanor together ran Todhunter School and started Val-Kill Industries.

While teaching at Todhunter School (above), Eleanor tried to give her students the kind of useful and exciting education Marie Souvestre (page 8) had given her.

Through her political connections, Eleanor made friends with two outspoken Democrats, Nancy Cook and Marion Dickerman. Nancy and Marion moved into Eleanor's cottage, Val-Kill, and in 1926 the three bought Todhunter School, a girls' school in New York City. Eleanor taught American history, drama and literature. Her students adored her.

The next year, Eleanor, Nancy and Marion opened Val-Kill Industries in a building near Eleanor's cottage. The company produced beautiful furniture and gave local people crafting skills to help them add to their incomes.

In 1928, FDR campaigned to become governor of New York state. To prove his polio hadn't made him too weak to take on the job, he put in long hours. FDR also made it a rule that he was never to be photographed while in his wheelchair or being carried. Eleanor didn't have much time to help his campaign — she was working too hard as co-chair of the National Women's Committee of the Democratic party.

When the votes were counted, FDR had won, but just barely. Eleanor unhappily prepared to move back to Albany, New York. She knew she'd have to stay in the background now that she was a governor's wife. Anything she said or did would be reported in the newspapers and would reflect on Franklin.

But soon Eleanor and all of North America had something much bigger to worry them. On October 24, 1929, a sudden crash in the stock market closed factories and threw millions out of work. The Great Depression hit New York state especially hard because industry was so important there.

In those days, there was no government welfare or unemployment insurance. When people lost their jobs, they had nowhere to turn for help. Both Eleanor and FDR believed it was important for government to take care of people. Fortunately, many people in New York state agreed. In 1930, FDR was easily re-elected as governor.

Because of FDR's success in New York state, no one was surprised when, in 1932, the Democratic party asked him to run for president of the United States. He campaigned hard, promising "a New Deal" to improve the country's economy. Eleanor helped organize the activities of the Democrats' women's division. FDR was elected president by a landslide.

Eleanor was happy for Franklin. But becoming First Lady would mean the end of any independent life for her.

After his polio attack, FDR wore leg braces (you can see them around his ankles). When he became governor of New York state on January 1, 1929, he posed with Eleanor (left) and his mother, Sara.

"You gain strength, courage, and confidence by every experience in which you really stop to look fear in the face ..."
— Eleanor Roosevelt

About 15 million people — a third of all American workers — were unemployed during the Great Depression. To help them, charities opened "soup kitchens" serving free meals.

Eleanor made the governor's mansion in Albany, New York, a lively place. Her children, including John (standing), and grandchildren, such as Anna's daughter, Sistie (on Franklin's knee), loved spending time there.

Val-Kill Industries made top-quality replicas of early American furniture.

First Lady

"There isn't going to be any First Lady. There is just going to be plain, ordinary Mrs. Roosevelt. And that's all."

— Eleanor Roosevelt

Although FDR is in the driver's seat, this is actually Eleanor's car. Because of his polio, FDR could only drive cars with special hand controls.

Although Eleanor dreaded being First Lady — having to give up her independence and attend formal teas and other events — she warmly greeted thousands at the White House. No one had ever seen a First Lady like Eleanor. She insisted on running the elevator herself, rather than waiting for an operator.

Eleanor's friend Lorena Hickok, a reporter, helped her adjust to her new life. Lorena also suggested Eleanor hold press conferences just for female journalists. This helped women because newspapers and radio stations had to hire a woman if they wanted reports on Eleanor's talks.

Because Franklin's polio made it difficult for him to get around, Eleanor became his legs and eyes. During 1933, she traveled 64 440 km (40 000 mi.) to see how Americans were coping with the Great Depression. Franklin taught her that at hospitals or prisons, it wasn't enough to check the menu. She was to peek into the pots to see what was really being cooked.

Eleanor sent Franklin so many memos that he set a limit of three a night. She prodded him to create the National Youth Administration to help young people during the Depression. She also pushed for the building of a new commuity, Arthurdale, to help poor miners in West Virginia. Seeing that Eleanor truly cared, the public sent her more than 300 000 letters asking for help.

Soon after FDR became president, thousands of World War I veterans marched to Washington. The marchers had been promised a bonus sometime in the future, but they didn't want to wait any longer. This was the second time the men had come to the capital city. When they'd arrived a year earlier, Herbert Hoover, who was president at the time, sent soldiers to get rid of them.

This time, Eleanor chatted with the veterans and talked about them at a press conference. Because of this, the public developed sympathy for the men. One veteran said, "Hoover sent the Army. Roosevelt sent his wife."

In 1936, FDR campaigned for re-election. Whenever he spoke, crowds demanded to see Eleanor, too. Sometimes people cheered more loudly for her than for him. FDR won the election by one of the largest margins ever. Eleanor would be staying in the White House.

Air travel was new when Eleanor was First Lady. In the 1920s and 1930s, Eleanor flew more miles than any woman in the world.

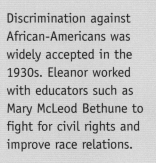

During the presidential campaign, Eleanor met reporter Lorena Hickok. Eleanor confided to "Hick" all her fears about being First Lady.

Discrimination against African-Americans was widely accepted in the 1930s. Eleanor worked with educators such as Mary McLeod Bethune to fight for civil rights and improve race relations.

These are the people of Arthurdale. The town opened in 1933 and was exactly the kind of project Eleanor loved. (Find out more about Arthurdale on page 32.)

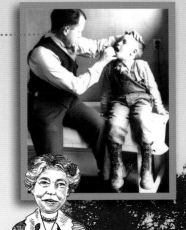

My Uncle Theodore was the first to call the president's home the White House.

Eleanor and Franklin turned the White House into an informal place. They made many changes, including adding a swimming pool — swimming was Franklin's only exercise.

Civil rights fighter

"There is so much to do, so many engrossing challenges, so many heartbreaking and pressing needs, so much in every day that is profoundly interesting."

— Eleanor Roosevelt

My Day ...By Eleanor Roosevelt

WASHINGTON: The judicial reception was held Tuesday night. The justices of the Supreme Court always head the line on this occasion and the chief justice always impresses me as looking the part so satisfactorily. He has great dignity, and I always get a sense of pleasure whenever I see Mrs. Hughes. I have never known her very well but I have known her now for a great many years.

I think the saying that as we grow older we all have exactly the beauty we deserve, applies admirably to her. As Mrs. Hughes has grown older her beauty has increased and her expression is very lovely.

A memorial service was held at 10:30 for Allee S. Freed, who died yesterday at the Emergency Hospital here. He has done a great deal to help us with the homesteads at Arthurdale and with the problems arising in other similar groups. His main interest was in housing.

I want to tell you today of a protest which has come to me from an association of architects who feel that architects were unjustly criticized when I made the suggestion that the advice of a woman valuable in every architect's office.

I said as a criticism of the profession. However, I ... not mean what ... believe a woman's advice would be useful in planning the interior of a room because it naturally affects both the exterior ways supposed ... arrangements of doors, electric outlets, etc. She was expected to provide this advice, but in the case of a large scale, individual women cannot be consulted, so it there is a field for the employment of trained women in ...

Eleanor's friend Lorena Hickok suggested Eleanor write the "My Day" column. It gave people a real view into the White House.

At the end of 1935, Eleanor began writing a popular newspaper column called "My Day." She told readers about her life in the White House, her travels and the people she met. Eleanor also wrote articles and books setting out her point of view on women's rights, politics, race relations and more. She gave much of the money she earned to charity.

It was Eleanor's amazing energy that allowed her to write so much, as well as travel and give speeches. She was an incredibly fast walker who left most people gasping to keep up. Sitting still was difficult for Eleanor — when chatting with someone, she usually knitted, too.

Eleanor's children also required her energy. They had problems in their personal lives and careers, going through many divorces and jobs. Eleanor sympathized but didn't want to interfere the way her mother-in-law had.

Civil rights were becoming very important to Eleanor, as she heard more and more stories of discrimination. For instance, in 1939, the wonderful African-American opera singer Marian Anderson was scheduled to perform at Constitution Hall in Washington. It was the capital's only building large enough for the concert.

But the building was owned by the Daughters of the American Revolution (DAR), women whose ancestors had fought in the Revolutionary War. The DAR said Marian couldn't sing at their hall because she was African-American.

When Eleanor heard this, she resigned from the DAR because of its racist stand. Then she helped organize an even bigger concert. Marian Anderson performed at the Lincoln Memorial for more than 75 000 people.

Also in 1939, Eleanor attended a meeting in Birmingham, Alabama. In southern states, Black people and White people had to sit on opposite sides of the hall — it was illegal to sit together. Eleanor didn't want to break the law, but she hated segregation. So she placed her chair in the middle of the aisle separating the two sides.

Because Eleanor wasn't afraid to speak her mind and take action, she had enemies. Some people criticized her opinions, while others made fun of her big teeth and unfashionable clothes. "Every woman in public life needs to develop skin as tough as rhinoceros hide," was Eleanor's response.

Angel food cake was one of Eleanor's favorite desserts, and she served it often at the White House.

I liked to begin my busy day with a horseback ride.

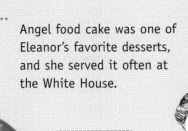

Eleanor was pleased by visits from her daughter, Anna, and Anna's son, John.

Meeting Americans where they lived and worked was important to Eleanor. Here she is visiting a nursery school in Des Moines, Iowa.

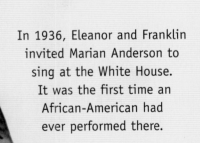

In 1936, Eleanor and Franklin invited Marian Anderson to sing at the White House. It was the first time an African-American had ever performed there.

World at war

"If we don't make this a more decent world to live in, I don't see how we can look these [soldiers] in the eyes."

— Eleanor Roosevelt

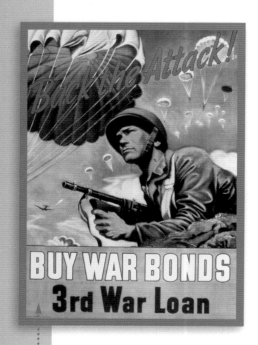

World War II was a hard time for Eleanor. All four of her sons were involved in the fighting, and Franklin didn't have the energy or time to listen to her ideas. Eleanor had to find new ways to be useful and keep busy.

In September 1939, Adolf Hitler's German troops invaded Poland, and so Britain and France declared war on Germany. World War II had begun, although the United States didn't immediately join the fighting. Eleanor hated war. But she also believed countries should be able to choose their own government and not be overrun by leaders such as Hitler.

In 1940, another American election was approaching. During this difficult time, many people felt the country needed a proven leader like FDR. But he'd already served two terms — no president had ever been elected three times. Despite this, FDR let the Democratic party know that if he was nominated for the 1940 election, he'd accept.

But many party members didn't like FDR's selection for vice-president. Then Eleanor spoke at a party convention. She reminded members how, during wartime, it was vital to pull together. Thanks to her, the party agreed to FDR's choice and gave him the nomination. Eleanor became the first president's wife to speak before a national party convention, and FDR went on to win the election.

The United States entered World War II in 1941, after Japanese planes bombed American naval ships in Pearl Harbor, Hawaii. Shortly before, Eleanor had been made co-director of the Office of Civilian Defense, an agency that prepared people at home for war. Almost immediately, she was attacked for her policies. People who felt they couldn't criticize FDR picked on Eleanor instead. In early 1942, she resigned.

Later that year, Eleanor flew to England to encourage American soldiers stationed there. The next year, she visited troops in the South Pacific. Spring 1944 saw Eleanor in the Caribbean and Central and South America.

In July, the Democratic party again asked FDR to run for president. He won an amazing fourth term that November. But his health wasn't good, and as the war drew to a close, it got worse. On April 12, 1945, in Warm Springs, Georgia, Franklin died.

Eleanor flew to Warm Springs to bring Franklin's body back to Washington. Despite her long-time hurt over his affair with Lucy Mercer, she'd depended on Franklin and was very sad. Eleanor was devastated to discover that Lucy and Franklin had met often, and that Lucy was with him when he died.

Eleanor thought her public life was finished. But she was wrong.

When Eleanor toured the South Pacific, the troops were told they were going to be visited by a woman. Eleanor was nervous, thinking that they'd expect a movie star and be disappointed by her. Instead they loved meeting the First Lady.

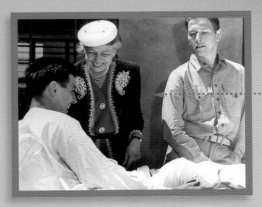

After Eleanor's visit to his troops, one officer said, "She alone had accomplished more good than any other person or any group of civilians who had passed through my area."

I always worked for peace, but I also felt that Hitler had to be stopped.

Franklin was buried at Hyde Park, New York. Soldiers, sailors and marines lined the route his casket traveled.

In February 1945, FDR (center) met with the leaders of the other two main countries fighting Germany, Prime Minister Winston Churchill of Great Britain (left) and Marshal Joseph Stalin of the Soviet Union (now called Russia).

The Globe

ROOSEVELT DEAD

Stroke Fatal at Co
Coalition Cabinet

9th Army, Over Elbe, Prepares Final Drive

Truman Takes Office Oath as President

Eleanor's United Nations

"My philosophy has been that if you have work to do and do it to the best of your ability you will not have much time to think about yourself."

— Eleanor Roosevelt

When Eleanor traveled, she took as little luggage as possible and always carried her own bag.

Eleanor missed Franklin and the power she'd enjoyed as First Lady. But the new president, Harry Truman, asked her to be one of the five American delegates to the first meeting of the United Nations (UN).

Having no experience in international affairs, Eleanor hesitated. She knew her performance could decide whether a woman would be appointed again. Despite her concerns, Eleanor agreed.

The other American delegates — all men — didn't think much of Eleanor. They assigned her to what they thought would be an unimportant committee: the one dealing with culture, education and human rights.

But Eleanor's group, the United Nations Human Rights Commission, became one of the most important. It had to decide what to do with all the refugees created by World War II. The United States believed refugees should be allowed to choose where to live, while the Soviet Union (now called Russia) felt they should go back to their homelands.

The head of the Soviet delegation was a great lawyer and a fiery speaker. Eleanor was scared to speak against him, but she made her speech without notes, as usual. A long speech by the Soviet delegate followed. Then the UN members voted — and Eleanor's side won. One of the American delegates said, "I want to say that I take back everything I ever said about her, and believe me it's been plenty."

After this success, Eleanor was elected chair of the UN's Human Rights Commission in 1946. The group's goal was to create an international bill of human rights. For two years, she skillfully directed the 18 people in her group, sometimes making them work 16-hour days.

On December 10, 1948, the Universal Declaration of Human Rights was approved by the United Nations. Then all the members rose to give Eleanor a standing ovation — an honor that had never happened before and hasn't happened since.

Eleanor worked for the United Nations until 1952, when the United States elected a new president, Dwight Eisenhower. Unlike Eleanor, he was a Republican, so he didn't re-appoint her to the UN. But Eleanor believed strongly in world peace and chose to volunteer for the American Association for the United Nations.

Eleanor moved out of the White House saying, "The story is over." She was happy to live at her beloved Val-Kill but said she did not want to stop being useful.

In 1946, Eleanor lost her front teeth in a car accident and had to have them replaced.

The flag of the United Nations shows the world surrounded by olive branches, a symbol of peace.

Eleanor was known as one of the hardest-working, best-prepared delegates at the United Nations.

The Universal Declaration of Human Rights was approved on December 10, 1948. Now that date is celebrated each year as Human Rights Day.

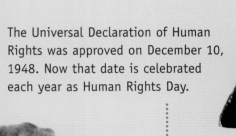

THE UNIVERSAL DECLARATION OF **Human Rights**

After I left the United Nations, I had time for more travel. Here I am in Japan.

First Lady of the World

In 1954, Eleanor celebrated her 70th birthday. She still had incredible energy, and the next year she traveled to Japan, Bali, Indonesia, Thailand and Cambodia. She toured the Soviet Union in 1957, returned the next year and also visited Morocco. Later, she flew to Israel and Iran. "I am willing to slow down," she said, "but I just don't know how."

At home in Val-Kill, Eleanor welcomed many visitors — not just family and friends but also politicians and world leaders. She was still an important person in the Democratic party and continued to top polls as America's most admired woman. About 100 letters flooded in to Eleanor each day.

The next president was John F. Kennedy, elected in 1960. A Democrat, President Kennedy recognized Eleanor's importance to his political party and country and asked her to take on a number of jobs. In 1961, he reappointed her to the American delegation to the United Nations. Later that year, he made Eleanor a member of the National Advisory Committee of the Peace Corps.

There was more to come. The president appointed Eleanor chair of the President's Commission on the Status of Women. No wonder — Eleanor had helped open up many opportunities for women. In April 1962, she spoke at a congressional hearing in favor of women being paid as much as men for doing the same job.

By the summer of 1962, Eleanor was almost 78. Her health deteriorated, and she spent a lot of time in hospital. Doctors did what they could, but she grew weaker and suffered from severe coughing and a high fever. She died on November 7, 1962, from a rare form of tuberculosis of the bone.

People across the United States and around the world mourned her loss. Eleanor had become a symbol of independence and political action, especially for women. She accomplished an amazing amount, yet always had time to talk with everyone. Many people feel that Eleanor's beliefs and actions made her a woman ahead of her time. She would probably have said she just used common sense.

With the courage to take action and the energy to take risks, Eleanor spoke out whenever she saw injustices. She thought for herself and knew what was important to her. Eleanor still influences the way people, both men and women, act and think today.

"Learn from the mistakes of others," Eleanor said. "You can't live long enough to make them all yourself."

Eleanor and Helen Keller, the deaf and blind woman who accomplished so much for people with disabilities, greatly admired each other. Here, Helen is feeling Eleanor's face so that she can "hear" what Eleanor is saying.

President John F. Kennedy visited Eleanor at Val-Kill to patch up a political disagreement. She received him graciously — but sat in a taller chair so she could talk down to him and make herself appear more powerful!

Eleanor's children and grandchildren visited her often. Some of her children became politicians, while her son Elliott wrote mystery books featuring Eleanor as a detective.

Because of Eleanor, the role of First Lady took on more importance for Americans. Around the world, she became famous for her kindness and courage.

"… remember that every step forward is the result of somebody who dreamed dreams."

— Eleanor Roosevelt

Appearing on TV, writing books and her newspaper column, speaking on radio — Eleanor did all these things until shortly before her death.

Eleanor's life at a glance

1882   January 30 — Franklin Delano Roosevelt is born in Hyde Park, New York

1884   October 11 — Eleanor Roosevelt is born in New York, New York

1892   December 7 — Eleanor's mother, Anna Hall Roosevelt, dies of diphtheria. Eleanor and her brothers go to live with their Grandmother Hall.

1894   August 14 — Elliott Roosevelt, Eleanor's father, dies of alcoholism

1899   Eleanor enrolls at Allenswood school near London, England

1902   Eleanor makes her society debut in New York City

1903   Eleanor begins teaching fitness at the Rivington Street Settlement House. She also joins the New York Consumers' League.

November — Eleanor becomes engaged to Franklin Delano Roosevelt

1905   March 17 — Eleanor marries Franklin in New York City

1906   May 3 — Eleanor gives birth to her first child, Anna

1907   December 23 — Eleanor's second child, James, is born

1909   March 18 — Eleanor gives birth to her third child, Franklin Jr.

November 1 — Franklin Jr. dies of pneumonia

1910   September 23 — Eleanor's fourth child, Elliott, is born

November — FDR is elected to the New York state senate

1913   FDR becomes Assistant Secretary of the Navy in Washington, D.C.

1914   August 1 — World War I begins

August 17 — Eleanor gives birth to her fifth child, Franklin Jr.

1916   March 13 — Eleanor's sixth and last child, John, is born

1917   April 6 — The United States enters World War I. Eleanor begins volunteer work related to the war.

1918   September — Eleanor learns of the affair between her husband and Lucy Mercer

November 11 — World War I ends

1920   Eleanor joins the League of Women Voters

1921   August — Franklin becomes paralyzed from polio

1922   Eleanor becomes a member of the Women's Trade Union League. She also joins the Women's Division of the New York State Democratic Committee.

1925   Franklin builds Val-Kill cottage for Eleanor at Hyde Park, New York

1926   Eleanor, Nancy Cook and Marion Dickerman purchase Todhunter School in New York City

1927   Eleanor opens a furniture factory, Val-Kill Industries, with Nancy and Marion

1928   Eleanor is appointed co-chair of the National Women's Committee of the Democratic party

FDR is elected governor of New York state

1929   October 24 — The Great Depression begins

1932   FDR is elected the 32nd president of the United States

1933   March 6 — Eleanor becomes the first wife of a president to hold all-female press conferences

She assists with the Arthurdale community project in West Virginia

1934 Eleanor pushes FDR to form the National Youth Administration

1935 Eleanor begins publishing her newspaper column, "My Day"

1936 FDR wins re-election as president

1939 April 9 — Eleanor helps arrange for African-American Marian Anderson to sing at the Lincoln Memorial in Washington, D.C.

Eleanor challenges segregation laws in Birmingham, Alabama

September 3 — World War II begins. The Great Depression ends.

1940 July 17 — Eleanor becomes the first president's wife to speak at the Democratic National Convention. That helps FDR win a third term as president.

1941 September — Eleanor is made co-director of the Office of Civilian Defense

December 7 — The United States enters World War II

1942 February — Eleanor resigns from the Office of Civilian Defense

October — Eleanor travels to England to encourage U.S. soldiers posted there

1943 Eleanor visits soldiers in the South Pacific

1944 Eleanor visits troops in the Caribbean and Central and South America

FDR is elected president for the fourth time

1945 April 12 — Franklin dies of a cerebral hemorrhage (bleeding in the brain) in Warm Springs, Georgia

September 2 — World War II ends

December — Eleanor becomes an American delegate to the United Nations

1946 Eleanor is elected chair of the United Nations Human Rights Commission

1948 December 10 — The United Nations passes the Universal Declaration of Human Rights, written by Eleanor's commission

1952 Eleanor resigns from the United Nations. She travels to Lebanon, Jordan, Israel, Pakistan and India.

1953– 1959 Eleanor travels the world, visiting many countries, including Japan, Greece, Bali, Thailand, Cambodia, the Soviet Union, Morocco and Iran

1961 President John F. Kennedy reappoints Eleanor to the American delegation to the United Nations. He also makes her a member of the National Advisory Committee of the Peace Corps.

1962 April — As chair of the Commission on the Status of Women, Eleanor speaks at a congressional hearing

November 7 — Eleanor dies of a rare, incurable form of tuberculosis of the bone in New York City

"Life has got to be lived — that's all there is to it."

Visit Eleanor

Arthurdale Heritage Museum, Arthurdale, West Virginia

At this museum, you can find out all about the community that Eleanor encouraged Franklin to build. You'll also see buildings set up to look as they did in the 1930s.

Eleanor Roosevelt National Historic Site, 4097 Albany Post Road, Hyde Park, New York

This is the only national monument to a First Lady. Val-Kill Industries closed during the Great Depression, and Eleanor renovated the factory to make it her home. You can tour it and walk through her gardens. There are also displays about Eleanor at the nearby Franklin D. Roosevelt Presidential Library and Museum.

Roosevelt Campobello International Park, Campobello Island, New Brunswick, Canada

Eleanor called Campobello Island "this quietest of places." She spent many summers here after she married Franklin. Visit the Roosevelts' 34-room summer home, where you'll see furniture and other items Eleanor and her family used.

You can see statues of Franklin and me at the Franklin Delano Roosevelt Memorial in Washington, D.C.

Index